THE AUSTRO-HUNGARIAN QUESTION.

CORRESPONDENCE

BETWEEN

MR. HÜLSEMANN,

AUSTRIAN CHARGÉ D'AFFAIRES,

AND

MR. WEBSTER,

SECRETARY OF STATE OF THE UNITED STATES.

WASHINGTON:
PRINTED BY GIDEON AND CO.
1851.

CORRESPONDENCE.

In Senate of the United States,
December 30, 1850.

A message was received from the President of the United States, by Mr. M. P. Fillmore, his private secretary, dated the 30th instant, communicating, in reply to a resolution of the Senate of the 20th instant, certain correspondence between our Government and Austria. The correspondence was read, and is as follows:

Department of State,
Washington, *December* 30, 1850.

To the President of the United States:

The Secretary of State, to whom has been referred the resolution of the Senate of the 26th instant, requesting the President "to communicate to the Senate, if not incompatible with the public interest, copies of any correspondence, if any has taken place, between the Department of State and the Austrian Chargé d'Affaires, respecting the appointment or proceedings of the agent sent out to examine and report upon the condition and prospects of the Hungarian people, during their recent struggle for independence," has the honor to lay before the President a copy of the correspondence called for by the resolution.

Respectfully submitted,
DANIEL WEBSTER.

Chevalier J. G. Hülsemann to the Secretary of State.

[Translation.]

AUSTRIAN LEGATION,
WASHINGTON, *September* 30, 1850.

The undersigned, Chargé d'Affaires of his Majesty the Emperor of Austria, has been instructed to make the following communication to the Secretary of State:

As soon as the Imperial Government became aware of the fact that a United States agent had been despatched to Vienna, with orders to watch for a favorable moment to recognise the Hungarian Republic, and to conclude a treaty of commerce with the same, the undersigned was directed to address some confidential but pressing representations to the Cabinet of Washington against that proceeding, which is so much at variance with those principles of international law, so scrupulously adhered to by Austria at all times and under all circumstances, towards the United States. In fact, how is it possible to reconcile such a mission with the principle of non-intervention, so formally announced by the United States as the basis of American policy, and which had just been sanctioned with so much solemnity by the President, in his inaugural address of March 5, 1849? Was it in return for the friendship and confidence which Austria had never ceased to manifest towards them, that the United States became so impatient for the downfall of the Austrian Monarchy, and even sought to accelerate that event by the utterance of their wishes to that effect? Those who did not hesitate to assume the responsibility of sending Mr. Dudley Mann on such an errand, should, independent of considerations of propriety, have borne in mind that they were exposing their emissary to be treated as a spy. It is to be regretted that the American Government was not better informed as to the actual resources of Austria, and her historical perseverance in defending her just rights. A knowledge of those resources would have led to the conclusion that a contest of a few months' duration could neither have exhausted the energies of that Power, nor turned aside its purpose to put down the insurrection. Austria has struggled against the French revolution for twenty-five years; the courage and perseverance which she exhibited in that memorable contest have been appreciated by the whole world.

To the urgent representations of the undersigned, Mr. Clayton answered that Mr. Mann's mission had no other object in view than to obtain reliable information as to the true state of affairs in Hungary, by personal observation; this explanation can hardly be admitted, for it says very little as to the cause of the anxiety which was felt to ascertain the chances of the revolutionists. Unfortunately, the language in which Mr. Mann's instructions were drawn gives us a very correct idea of their scope. This language was offensive to the Imperial Cabinet, for it designates the Austrian Government as an *iron rule*, and represents the rebel chief, Kossuth, as an illustrious man; while improper expressions are introduced in regard to Russia, the intimate and faithful ally of Austria. Notwithstanding these hostile demonstrations, the Imperial Cabinet has deemed it proper to preserve a conciliatory deportment, making ample allowance for the ignorance of the Cabinet of Washington on the subject of Hungarian affairs, and its disposition to give credence to the mendacious rumors which are propagated by the American press. This extremely painful incident, therefore, might have been passed over without any written evidence being left, on our part, in the archives of the United States, had not General Taylor thought proper to revive the whole subject by communicating to the Senate, in his message of the 18th of last March, the instructions with which Mr. Mann had been furnished on the occasion of his mission to Vienna. The publicity which has been given to that document has placed the Imperial Government under the necessity of entering a formal protest, through its official representative, against the proceedings of the American Government, lest that Government should construe our silence into approbation, or toleration even, of the principles which appear to have guided its action and the means it has adopted.

In view of all these circumstances, the undersigned has been instructed to declare that the Imperial Government totally disapproves, and will always continue to disapprove, of those proceedings, so offensive to the laws of propriety; and that it protests against all interference in the internal affairs of its Government. Having thus fulfilled his duty, the undersigned considers it a fortunate circumstance that he has it in his power to assure the Secretary of State that the Imperial Government is disposed to cultivate relations of friendship and good understanding with the United States, relations which may have been momentarily weakened, but which could not again be seriously disturbed without placing the cardinal interests of the two countries in jeopardy.

The instructions for addressing this communication to Mr. Clayton reached Washington at the time of General Taylor's death. In compliance with the requisitions of propriety, the undersigned deemed it his duty to defer the task until the new administration had been completely organized; a delay which he now rejoices at, as it has given him the opportunity of ascertaining from the new President himself, on the occasion of the reception of the diplomatic corps, that the fundamental policy of the United States, so frequently proclaimed, would guide the relations of the American Government with the other Powers. Even if the Government of the United States were to think it proper to take an indirect part in the political movements of Europe, American policy would be exposed to acts of retaliation, and to certain inconveniences, which could not fail to affect the commerce and the industry of the two hemispheres. All countries are obliged, at some period or other, to struggle against internal difficulties; all forms of government are exposed to such disagreeable episodes; the United States have had some experience in this very recently. Civil war is a possible occurrence every where, and the encouragement which is given to the spirit of insurrection and of disorder most frequently falls back upon those who seek to aid it in its developments, in spite of justice and wise policy.

The undersigned avails himself of this occasion to renew to the Secretary of State the assurance of his distinguished consideration.

HÜLSEMANN.

To the Hon. DANIEL WEBSTER,
Secretary of State of the United States.

The Secretary of State to Mr. Hülsemann.

DEPARTMENT OF STATE,
WASHINGTON, *December* 21, 1850.

The undersigned, Secretary of State of the United States, had the honor to receive, some time ago, the note of Mr. Hülsemann, Chargé d'Affaires of his Majesty, the Emperor of Austria, of the 30th September. Causes, not arising from any want of personal regard for Mr. Hülsemann, or of proper respect for his Government, have delayed an answer until the present moment. Having submitted Mr. Hülsemann's letter to the President, the undersigned is now directed by him to return the following reply.

The objects of Mr. Hülsemann's note are, first, to protest, by order of his Government, against the steps taken by the late President of the United States to ascertain the progress and probable result of the revolutionary movements in Hungary; and, secondly, to complain of some expressions in the instructions of the late Secretary of State to Mr. A. Dudley Mann, a confidential agent of the United States, as communicated by President Taylor to the Senate on the 28th of March last.

The principal ground of protest is founded on the idea, or in the allegation, that the Government of the United States, by the mission of Mr. Mann, and his instructions, has interfered in the domestic affairs of Austria in a manner unjust or disrespectful toward that Power. The President's message was a communication made by him to the Senate, transmitting a correspondence between the Executive Government and a confidential agent of its own. This would seem to be itself a domestic transaction, a mere instance of intercourse between the President and the Senate, in the manner which is usual and indispensable in communications between the different branches of the Government. It was not addressed either to Austria or Hungary; nor was it any public manifesto, to which any foreign State was called on to reply. It was an account of its transactions communicated by the Executive Government to the Senate, at the request of that body; made public, indeed, but made public only because such is the common and usual course of proceeding; and it may be regarded as somewhat strange, therefore, that the Austrian Cabinet did not perceive that, by the instructions given to Mr. Hülsemann, it was itself interfering with the domestic concerns of a foreign State, the very thing which is the ground of its complaint against the United States.

This Department has, on former occasions, informed the Ministers of Foreign Powers that a communication from the President to either House of Congress is regarded as a domestic communication, of which, ordinarily, no foreign State has cognizance; and, in more recent instances, the great inconvenience of making such communications subjects of diplomatic correspondence and discussion has been fully shown. If it had been the pleasure of his Majesty the Emperor of Austria, during the struggles in Hungary, to have admonished the Provisional Government or the people of that country against involving themselves in disaster, by following the evil and dangerous example of the United States of America in making efforts for the establishment of independent Governments, such an admonition from that Sovereign to his Hungarian subjects, would not have originated here a diplomatic correspondence. The President might, perhaps, on this ground, have declined to direct any particular reply to Mr. Hülsemann's note; but, out of proper respect for the Austrian Government, it has been thought better to answer that note at length; and the more especially, as the occasion is not unfavorable for the expression of the general sentiments of the Government of the United States upon the topics which that note discusses.

A leading subject in Mr. Hülsemann's note, is that of the correspondence between Mr. Hülsemann and the predecessor of the undersigned, in which Mr. Clayton, by direction of the President, informed Mr. Hülsemann "that Mr. Mann's mission had no other object in view than to obtain reliable information as to the true state of affairs in Hungary, by personal observation." Mr. Hülsemann remarks, that "this explanation can hardly be admitted, for it says very little as to the cause of the anxiety which was felt to ascertain the chances of the revolutionists." As this, however, is the only purpose which can, with any appearance of truth, be attributed to the agency; as nothing whatever is alleged by Mr. Hülsemann to have been either done or said by the agent inconsistent with such an object, the undersigned conceives that Mr. Clayton's explanation ought to be deemed not only admissible, but quite satisfactory. Mr. Hülsemann states, in the course of his note, that his instructions to address his present communication to Mr. Clayton reached Washington about the time of the lamented death of the late President, and that he delayed from a sense of propriety the execution of his task until the new Administration should be fully organized: "a delay which he now rejoices at, as it has given him the opportunity of ascertaining from the new President himself, on the occasion of the reception of the diplomatic corps, that the fundamental policy of the United States, so frequently proclaimed, would guide the relations of the American Government with other powers." Mr. Hülsemann also observes that it is in his power to assure the undersigned "that the Imperial Government is disposed to cultivate relations of friendship and good understanding with the United States." The President receives this assurance of the disposition of the Imperial Government with great satisfaction, and, in consideration of the friendly relations of the two Governments thus mutually recognised, and of the peculiar nature of the incidents by which their good understanding is supposed by Mr. Hülsemann to have been, for a moment, disturbed or endangered, the President regrets that Mr. Hülsemann did not feel himself at liberty wholly to forbear from the execution of instructions, which were of course transmitted from Vienna without any foresight of the state of things under which they would reach Washington. If Mr. Hülsemann saw in the address of the President to the diplomatic corps, satisfactory pledges of the sentiments and the policy of this Government, in regard to neutral rights and neutral duties, it might, perhaps, have been better not to bring on a discussion of past transactions. But the undersigned readily admits that this was a question fit only for the consideration and decision of Mr. Hülsemann himself; and although the President does not see that any good purpose can be answered by re-opening the inquiry into the propriety of the steps taken by President Taylor, to ascertain the probable issue of the late civil war in Hungary, justice to his memory requires the undersigned briefly to re-state the history of those steps, and to show their consistency with the neutral policy which has invariably guided the Government of the United States in its foreign relations, as well as with the established and well-settled principles of national intercourse, and the doctrines of public law.

The undersigned will first observe that the President is persuaded, His Majesty the Emperor of Austria, does not think that the Government of the United States ought to view, with unconcern, the extraordinary events which have occurred, not only in his dominions, but in many other parts of Europe, since February, 1848. The Government and people of the United States, like other intelligent governments and communities, take a lively interest in the movements and the events of this remarkable age, in whatever part of the world they may be exhibited. But the interest taken by the United States in those events, has not proceeded from any disposition to depart from that neutrality toward foreign Powers, which is among the deepest principles and the most cherished traditions of the political history of the Union. It has been the necessary effect of the unexampled character of the events themselves, which could not fail to arrest the attention of the contemporary world; as they will doubtless fill a memorable page in history. But the undersigned goes further, and freely admits that in proportion as these extraordinary events appeared to have their origin in those great ideas of responsible and popular governments, on which the American Constitutions themselves are wholly founded, they could not but command the warm sympathy of the people of this country.

Well known circumstances in their history, indeed their whole history, have made them the representatives of purely popular principles of government. In this light they now stand before the world. They could not, if they would, conceal their character, their condition, or their destiny. They could not, if they so desired, shut out from the view of mankind the causes which have placed them, in so short a national career, in the station which they now hold among the civilized States of the world. They could not, if they desired it, suppress either the thoughts or the hopes which arise in men's minds, in other countries, from contemplating their successful example of free government. That very intelligent and distinguished personage, the Emperor Joseph the Second, was among the first to discern this necessary consequence of the American Revolution on the sentiments and opinions of the people of Europe. In a letter to his Minister in the Netherlands in 1787, he observes that "it is remarkable that France, by the assistance which she afforded to the Americans, gave birth to reflections on freedom." This fact, which the sagacity of that monarch perceived at so early a day, is now known and admitted by intelligent Powers all over the world. True, indeed, it is, that the prevalence on the other continent of sentiments favorable to republican liberty, is the result of the re-action of America upon Europe; and the source and centre of this re-action has doubtless been, and now is, in these United States. The position thus belonging to the United States is a fact as inseparable from their history, their constitutional organization, and their character, as the opposite position of the Powers composing the European alliance is from the history and constitutional organization of the Government of those Powers. The sovereigns who form that alliance have not unfrequently felt it their right to interfere with the political movements of foreign States; and have, in their manifestoes and declarations, denounced the popular ideas of the age in terms so comprehensive as of necessity to include the United States, and their forms of government. It is well known that one of the leading principles announced by the allied sovereigns, after the restoration of the Bourbons, is, that all popular or constitutional rights are holden no otherwise than as grants and indulgences from crowned heads. "Useful and necessary changes in legislation and administration," says the Laybach Circular of May, 1821, "ought only to emanate from the free will and intelligent conviction of those whom God has rendered responsible for power; all that deviates from this line necessarily leads to disorder, commotions, and evils far more insufferable than those which they pretend to remedy." And his late Austrian Majesty, Francis I, is reported to have declared in an address to the Hungarian Diet, in 1820, that "the whole world had become foolish, and, leaving their ancient laws, was in search of imaginary constitutions." These declarations amount to nothing less than a denial of the lawfulness of the origin of the Government of the United States, since it is certain that that Government was established in consequence of a change which did not proceed from thrones, or the permission of crowned heads. But the Government of the United States heard these denunciations of its fundamental principles without remonstrance, or the disturbance of its equanimity. This was thirty years ago.

The power of this Republic, at the present moment, is spread over a region, one of the richest and most fertile on the globe, and of an extent in comparison with which the possessions of the House of Hapsburg are but as a patch on the earth's surface. Its population, already twenty-five millions, will exceed that of the Austrian empire within the period during which it may be hoped that Mr. Hülsemann may yet remain in the honorable discharge of his duties to his Government. Its navigation and commerce are hardly exceeded by the oldest and most commercial nations; its maritime means and its maritime power may be seen by Austria herself, in all seas where she has ports, as well as it may be seen, also, in all other quarters of the globe. Life, liberty, property, and all personal rights are amply secured to all citizens, and protected by just and stable laws; and credit, public and private, is as well established as in any government of Continental Europe. And the country, in all its interests and concerns, partakes most largely in all the improvements and progress which distinguish the age. Certainly, the United States may be pardoned, even by those who profess adherence to the principles of absolute governments, if they entertain an ardent affection for those popular forms of political organization which have so rapidly advanced their own prosperity and happiness, and enabled them, in so short a period, to bring their country and the hemisphere to which it belongs, to the notice and respectful regard, not to say the admiration, of the civilized world. Nevertheless, the United States have abstained, at all times, from acts of interference with the political changes of Europe. They cannot, however, fail to cherish always a lively interest in the fortunes of nations struggling for institutions like their own. But this sympathy, so far from being necessarily a hostile feeling toward any of the parties to these great national struggles, is quite consistent with amicable relations with them all. The Hungarian people are three or four times as numerous as the inhabitants of these United States were when the American Revolution broke out. They possess, in a distinct language, and in other respects, important elements of a separate nationality, which the Anglo-Saxon race in this country did not possess; and if the United States wish success to countries contending for popular constitutions and national independence, it is only because they regard such constitutions and such national independence, not as imaginary, but as real blessings. They claim no right, however, to take part in the struggles of foreign Powers in order to promote these ends. It is only in defence of his own Government, and its principles and character, that the undersigned has now expressed himself on this subject. But when the United States behold the people of foreign countries without any such interference, spontaneously moving toward the adoption of institutions like their own, it surely cannot be expected of them to remain wholly indifferent spectators.

In regard to the recent very important occurrences in the Austrian empire, the undersigned freely admits the difficulty which exists in this country, and is alluded to by Mr. Hülsemann, of obtaining accurate information. But this difficulty is by no means to be ascribed to what Mr. Hülsemann calls—with little justice, as it seems to the undersigned—"the mendacious rumors propagated by the American press." For information on this subject, and others of the same kind, the American press is, of necessity, almost wholly dependant upon that of Europe; and if "mendacious rumors" respecting Austrian and Hungarian affairs have been any where propagated, that propagation of falsehoods has been most prolific on the European continent, and in countries immediately bordering on the Austrian empire. But, wherever these errors may have originated, they certainly justified the late President in seeking true information through authentic channels. His attention was first particularly drawn to the state of things in Hungary, by the correspondence of Mr. Stiles, Chargé d'Affaires of the United States at Vienna. In the autumn of 1848, an application was made to this gentleman, on behalf of Mr. Kossuth, formerly Minister of Finance for the kingdom of Hungary by Imperial appointment, but at the time the application was made, Chief of the Revolutionary Government. The object of this application was to obtain the good offices of Mr. Stiles with the Imperial Government, with a view to the suspension of hostilities. This application became the subject of a conference between Prince Schwarzenberg, the Imperial Minister for Foreign Affairs, and Mr. Stiles. The Prince commended the considerateness and propriety with which Mr. Stiles had acted; and, so far from disapproving his interference, advised him, in case he received a further communication from the Revolutionary Government in Hungary, to have an interview with Prince Windischgrätz, who was charged by the Emperor with the proceedings determined on in relation to that kingdom. A week after these occurrences, Mr. Stiles received, through a secret channel, a communication signed by L. Kossuth, President of the Committee of Defence, and countersigned by Francis Pulsky, Secretary of State. On the receipt of this communication, Mr. Stiles had an interview with Prince Windischgrätz, "who received him with the utmost kindness, and thanked him for his efforts toward reconciling the existing difficulties." Such were the incidents which first drew the attention of the Government of the United States particularly to the affairs of Hungary, and the conduct of Mr. Stiles, though acting without instructions in a matter of much delicacy, having been viewed with satisfaction by the Imperial Government, was approved by that of the United States.

In the course of the year 1848, and in the early part of 1849, a considerable number of Hungarians came to the United States. Among them were individuals representing themselves to be in the confidence of the Revolutionary Government, and by these persons the President was strongly urged to recognise the existence of that Government. In these applications, and in the manner in which they were viewed bythe President, there was nothing unusual; still less was there anything unauthorized by the law of nations. It is the right of every independent State to enter into friendly relations with every other independent State. Of course, questions of prudence naturally arise in reference to new States, brought by successful revolutions into the family of nations; but it is not to be required of neutral Powers that they should await the recognition of the new Government by the parent State. No principle of public law has been more frequently acted upon, within the last thirty years, by the great Powers of the world than this. Within that period eight or ten new States have established independent Governments within the limits of the colonial dominions of Spain, on this continent; and in Europe the same thing has been done by Belgium and Greece. The existence of all these Governments was recognised by some of the leading Powers of Europe, as well as by the United States, before it was acknowledged by the States from which they had separated themselves. If, therefore, the United States had gone so far as formally to acknowledge the independence of Hungary, although, as the result has proved, it would have been a precipitate step, and one from which no benefit would have resulted to either party; it would not, nevertheless, have been an act against the law of nations, provided they took no part in her contest with Austria. But the United States did no such thing. Not only did they not yield to Hungary any actual countenance or succor; not only did they not show their ships of war in the Adriatic with any menacing or hostile aspect, but they studiously abstained from every thing which had not been done in other cases in times past, and contented themselves with instituting an inquiry into the truth and reality of alleged political occurrences. Mr. Hülsemann incorrectly states, unintentionally certainly, the nature of the mission of this agent, when he says that "a United States agent had been dispatched to Vienna with orders to watch for a favorable moment to recognise the Hungarian republic, and to conclude a treaty of commerce with the same." This, indeed, would have been a lawful object, but Mr. Mann's errand was, in the first instance, purely one of inquiry. He had no power to act, unless he had first come to the conviction that a firm and stable Hungarian Government existed. "The principal object the President has in view," according to his instructions, "is to obtain minute and reliable information in regard to Hungary in connexion with the affairs of adjoining countries, the probable issue of the present revolutionary movements, and the chances we may have of forming commercial arrangements with that Power favorable to the United States." Again, in the same paper, it is said: "The object of the President is to obtain information in regard to Hungary, and her resources and prospects, with a view to an early recognition of her independence and the formation of commercial relations with her." It was only in the event that the new Government should appear, in the opinion of the agent, to be firm and stable, that the President proposed to recommend its recognition.

Mr. Hülsemann, in qualifying these steps of President Taylor with the epithet of "hostile," seems to take for granted that the inquiry could, in the expectation of the President, have but one result, and that favorable to Hungary. If this were so, it would not change the case. But the American Government sought for nothing but truth; it desired to learn the facts through a reliable channel. It so happened, in the chances and vicissitudes of human affairs, that the result was adverse to the Hungarian revolution. The American agent, as was stated in his instructions to be not unlikely, found the condition of Hungarian affairs less prosperous than it had been, or had been believed to be. He did not enter Hungary, nor hold any direct communication with her revolutionary leaders. He reported against the recognition of her independence, because he found she had been unable to set up a firm and stable government. He carefully forbore, as his instructions required, to give publicity to his mission, and the undersigned supposes that the Austrian Government first learned its existence from the communications of the President to the Senate.

Mr. Hülsemann will observe from this statement that Mr.

Mann's mission was wholly unobjectionable, and strictly within the rule of the law of nations, and the duty of the United States as a neutral Power. He will accordingly feel how little foundation there is for his remark, that "those who did not hesitate to assume the responsibility of sending Mr. Dudley Mann on such an errand, should, independent of considerations of propriety, have borne in mind that they were exposing their emissary to be treated as a spy." A spy is a person sent by one belligerent to gain secret information of the forces and defences of the other, to be used for hostile purposes. According to practice, he may use deception, under the penalty of being lawfully hanged if detected. To give this odious name and character to a confidential agent of a neutral Power, bearing the commission of his country, and sent for a purpose fully warranted by the law of nations, is not only to abuse language, but also to confound all just ideas, and to announce the wildest and most extravagant notions, such as certainly were not to have been expected in a grave diplomatic paper; and the President directs the undersigned to say to Mr. Hülsemann, that the American Government would regard such an imputation upon it by the Cabinet of Austria, as that it employs spies, and that in a quarrel none of its own, as distinctly offensive, if it did not presume, as it is willing to presume, that the word used in the original German was not of equivalent meaning with "spy" in the English language, or that in some other way the employment of such an opprobrious term may be explained. Had the Imperial Government of Austria subjected Mr. Mann to the treatment of a spy, it would have placed itself without the pale of civilized nations; and the Cabinet of Vienna may be assured that if it had carried, or attempted to carry, any such lawless purpose into effect, in the case of an authorized agent of this Government, the spirit of the people of this country would have demanded immediate hostilities to be waged by the utmost exertion of the power of the Republic, military and naval.

Mr. Hülsemann proceeds to remark that "this extremely painful incident, therefore, might have been passed over, without any written evidence being left on our part in the archives of the United States, had not General Taylor thought proper to revive the whole subject, by communicating to the Senate, in his message of the 18th [28th] of last March, the instructions with which Mr. Mann had been furnished on the occasion of his mission to Vienna. The publicity which has been given to that document has placed the Imperial Government under the necessity of entering a formal protest, through its official representative, against the proceedings of the American Government, lest that Government should construe our silence into approbation, or toleration even, of the principles which appear to have guided its action and the means it has adopted." The undersigned re-asserts to Mr. Hülsemann, and to the Cabinet of Vienna, and in the presence of the world, that the steps taken by President Taylor, now protested against by the Austrian Government, were warranted by the law of nations and agreeable to the usages of civilized States. With respect to the communication of Mr. Mann's instructions to the Senate, and the language in which they are couched, it has already been said, and Mr. Hülsemann must feel the justice of the remark, that these are domestic affairs, in reference to which the Government of the United States cannot admit the slightest responsibility to the Government of his Imperial Majesty. No State, deserving the appellation of independent, can permit the language in which it may instruct its own officers in the discharge of their duties to itself to be called in question under any pretext by a foreign Power. But, even if this were not so, Mr. Hülsemann is in an error in stating that the Austrian Government is called an "Iron Rule" in Mr. Mann's instructions. That phrase is not found in the paper; and in respect to the honorary epithet bestowed in Mr. Mann's instructions on the late chief of the Revolutionary Government of Hungary, Mr. Hülsemann will bear in mind that the Government of the United States cannot justly be expected, in a confidential communication to its own agent, to withhold from an individual an epithet of distinction of which a great part of the world thinks him worthy, merely on the ground that his own Government regards him as a rebel. At an early stage of the American Revolution, while Washington was considered by the English Government as a rebel chief, he was regarded on the continent of Europe as an illustrious hero. But the undersigned will take the liberty of bringing the Cabinet of Vienna into the presence of its own predecessors, and of citing for its consideration the conduct of the Imperial Government itself. In the year 1777, the war of the American Revolution was raging all over these United States; England was prosecuting that war with a most resolute determination, and by the exertion of all her military means to the fullest extent. Germany was at that time at peace with England; and yet an agent of that Congress, which was looked upon by England in no other light than that of a body in open rebellion, was not only received with great respect by the Ambassador of the Empress Queen at Paris, and by the Minister of the Grand Duke of Tuscany, who afterwards mounted the imperial throne, but resided in Vienna for a considerable time; not, indeed, officially acknowledged, but treated with courtesy and respect; and the Emperor suffered himself to be persuaded by that agent to exert himself to prevent the German Powers from furnishing troops to England to enable her to suppress the rebellion in America. Neither Mr. Hülsemann, nor the cabinet of Vienna, it is presumed, will undertake to say that any thing said or done by this Government in regard to the recent war between Austria and Hungary is not borne out, and much more than borne out, by this example of the Imperial Court. It is believed that the Emperor Joseph the Second, habitually spoke in terms of respect and admiration of the character of Washington, as he is known to have done of that of Franklin; and he deemed it no infraction of neutrality to inform himself of the progress of the Revolutionary struggle in America, nor to express his deep sense of the merits and the talents of those illustrious men who were then leading their country to independence and renown. The undersigned may add, that in 1781, the Courts of Russia and Austria proposed a diplomatic Congress of the belligerent Powers, to which the Commissioners of the United States should be admitted.

Mr. Hülsemann thinks that in Mr. Mann's instructions, improper expressions are introduced in regard to Russia; but the undersigned has no reason to suppose that Russia herself is of that opinion. The only observation made in those instructions about Russia is that she "has chosen to assume an attitude of interference, and her immense preparations for invading and reducing the Hungarians to the rule of Austria, from which they desire to be released, gave so serious a character to the contest as to awaken the most painful solicitude in the minds of Americans." The undersigned cannot but consider the Austrian Cabinet as unnecessarily susceptible in looking upon language like this as a "hostile demonstration." If we remember that it was addressed by the Government to its own agent, and has received publicity only through a communication from one Department of the American Government to another, the language quoted must be deemed moderate and inoffensive. The comity of nations would hardly forbid its being addressed to the two Imperial Powers themselves. It is scarcely necessary for the undersigned to say, that the relations of the United States with Russia have always been of the most friendly kind, and have never been deemed by either party to require any compromise of their peculiar views upon subjects of domestic or foreign polity, or the true origin of Governments. At any rate, the fact that Austria, in her contest with Hungary, had an intimate and faithful ally in Russia, cannot alter the real nature of the question between Austria and Hungary, nor in any way affect the neutral rights and duties of the Government of the United States, or the justifiable sympathies of the American people. It is, indeed, easy to conceive, that favor toward struggling Hungary would be not diminished, but increased, when it was seen that the arm of Austria was strengthened and upheld by a Power whose assistance threatened to be, and which in the end proved to be, overwhelmingly destructive of all her hopes.

Toward the conclusion of his note Mr. Hülsemann remarks that "if the Government of the United States were to think it proper to take an indirect part in the political movements of Europe, American policy would be exposed to acts of retaliation, and to certain inconveniences which would not fail to affect the commerce and industry of the two hemispheres." As to this possible fortune, this hypothetical retaliation, the Government and people of the United States are quite willing to take their chances and abide their destiny. Taking neither a direct nor an indirect part in the domestic or intestine movements of Europe, they have no fear of events of the nature alluded to by Mr. Hülsemann. It would be idle now to discuss with Mr. Hülsemann those acts of retaliation which he imagines may possibly take place at some indefinite time hereafter. Those questions will be discussed when they arise; and Mr. Hülsemann and the Cabinet at Vienna may rest assured that, in the mean time, while performing with strict and exact fidelity all their neutral duties, nothing will deter either the Government or the people of the United States from exercising, at their own discretion, the rights belonging to them as an independent nation, and of forming and expressing their own opinions, freely and at all times, upon the great political events which may transpire among the civilized nations of the earth. Their own institutions stand upon the broadest principles of civil liberty; and believing those principles and the fundamental laws in which they are embodied to be eminently favorable to the prosperity of States—to be, in fact, the only principles of government which meet the demands of the present enlightened age—the President has perceived, with great satisfaction, that, in the Constitution recently introduced into the Austrian Empire, many of these great principles are recognised and applied, and he cherishes a sincere wish that they may produce the same happy effects throughout his Austrian Majesty's extensive dominions that they have done in the United States.

The undersigned has the honor to repeat to Mr. Hülsemann the assurance of his high consideration.

DAN'L WEBSTER.

www.ingramcontent.com/pod-product-compliance
Lightning Source LLC
LaVergne TN
LVHW011147110826
845150LV00008B/2554
9781418192358